AF428025

ISBN 979-8-9884492-3-2

For more Frisky Finn fun, visit www.danimartindalebooks.com.

Frisky Finn
Makes a Friend

It was a sunny day,
and Frisky Finn was ready to play.

But the ducks just bathed,
and the horses just ate.
Even the dogs just slept in late.

Then a truck and trailer came up the drive.
The animals ran to see who had arrived.

"What will it be?" asked Cathy, the cow.
"A bull just for me?"
"I bet it's a puppy," Rex's tail wagged with glee.

"What do you think it is?" asked Finn.
"Just wait and see," his mom said with a grin.

Out stepped a small beast on four hooves
Rex backed up and let out a few woofs.

"Hee-haw," the beast said hello.
The crowd's chatter began to grow.

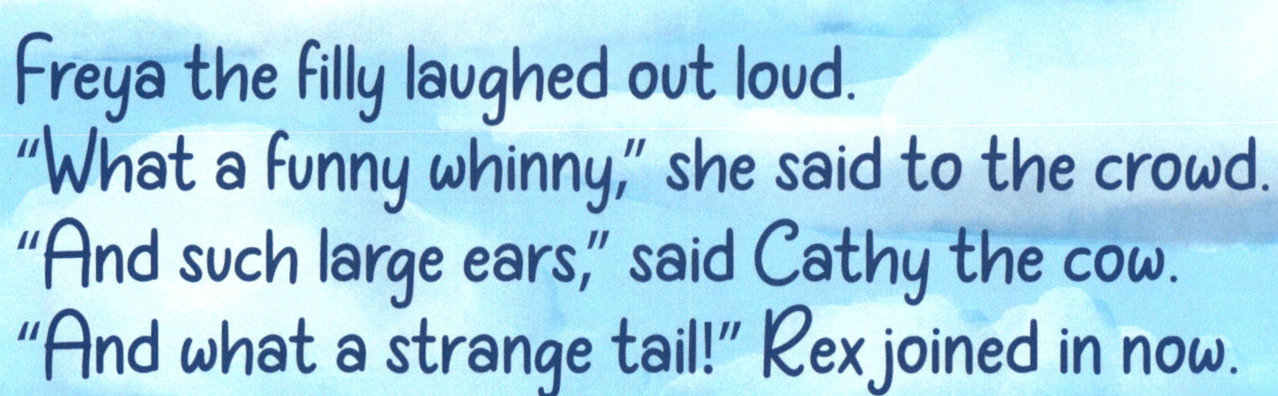

Freya the filly laughed out loud.
"What a funny whinny," she said to the crowd.
"And such large ears," said Cathy the cow.
"And what a strange tail!" Rex joined in now.

The donkey walked into the barn alone and sad.
His bray, he thought, really wasn't that bad.

The next day it was more of the same.
Being a donkey, it seemed,
brought nothing but shame.

Finn joined in. He just wanted to belong.
But deep inside, something felt wrong.

Finn asked, "Why can't the others be nice?"
"Why don't you stop it?" Mom offered advice.

Finn admitted, "I guess I'm scared."
"I'm sure he is too," his mom shared.

"But, Mom," said Finn. "Why does he have to look so silly? If he didn't, he could be friends with me and the filly!"

Mom asked, "What about Dylan, the duck?
Does he look like the herd?"
Finn shouted, "Silly Mom! He is a bird!"

Then Mom asked, "Does Freya look like you?"
Finn said, "Well not quite the same it's true."

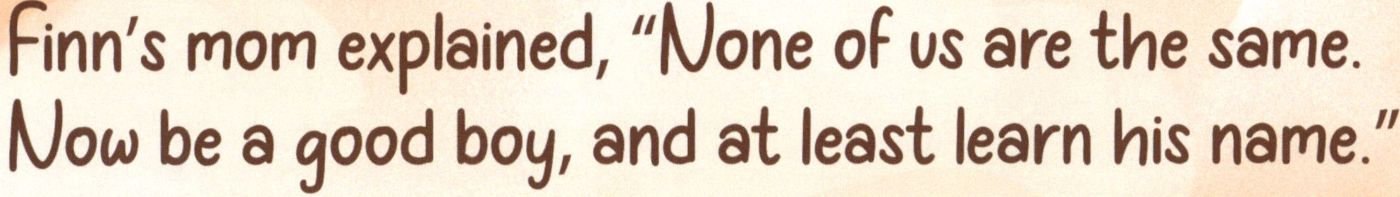

Finn's mom explained, "None of us are the same.
Now be a good boy, and at least learn his name."

Finn gave his mom's words some thought.
Being nice, he decided, wasn't asking a lot.

The next day he saw his chance.
The donkey gave a nervous glance.

"Hi, my name is Finn," he said with a grin.
"I'm Diego," the donkey said with care.
The other animals started to stare.

Dylan quacked, "Finn, why are you with this freak?"
Diego looked small and weak.
"Finn, have you gone mad?"
Freya said, "This looks quite bad."

Finn answered with courage, "It's bad to make fun of things you see just because they're different than you and me."

The group looked upset.
"We're sorry, Diego," they finally said with regret.

Diego took a minute.
Even a donkey has his limits.
But really, there was only one decision.
"Alright, you are all forgiven."

So, the animals learned to let
their differences go, and Finn gained
a new friend, a donkey named Diego.

www.ingramcontent.com/pod-product-compliance
Lightning Source LLC
Chambersburg PA
CBHW041454110726
48007CB00002B/18